About the Author

LAURA HAWRYLUCK received her MD from the University of Western Ontario where she served her Internal Medicine residency. She completed a Fellowship in Critical Care at the University of Manitoba and MSc. in Bioethics from the University of Toronto, Canada. Professor of Critical Care Medicine at the University of Toronto, she was awarded the Queen's Golden Jubilee Medal for contributions to Canada in improving end of life care, the Medico-Legal Society of Toronto award for contributions to health law and the University of Toronto Interdepartmental Critical Care Medicine Humanitarian Award for her contributions to international humanitarian work.

Words That Matter

Dr Laura A. Hawryluck

Words That Matter

Olympia Publishers
London

www.olympiapublishers.com
OLYMPIA PAPERBACK EDITION

Copyright © Dr Laura A. Hawryluck 2021

The right of Dr Laura A. Hawryluck to be identified as author of this work has been asserted in accordance with sections 77 and 78 of the Copyright, Designs and Patents Act 1988.

All Rights Reserved

No reproduction, copy or transmission of this publication may be made without written permission.
No paragraph of this publication may be reproduced, copied or transmitted save with the written permission of the publisher, or in accordance with the provisions of the Copyright Act 1956 (as amended).

Any person who commits any unauthorised act in relation to this publication may be liable to criminal prosecution and civil claims for damage.

A CIP catalogue record for this title is available from the British Library.

ISBN: 978-1-78830-953-0

This is a work of fiction.
Names, characters, places and incidents originate from the writer's imagination. Any resemblance to actual persons, living or dead, is purely coincidental.

First Published in 2021

Olympia Publishers
Tallis House
2 Tallis Street
London
EC4Y 0AB

Printed in Great Britain

Dedication

To everyone who has 'been there' too — this one is for you.

Introduction

Words matter: they reveal who we are, to ourselves and others. I wrote this book using verse to speak about some of the more challenging inter-personal moments that we all struggle with, as we live with people we love and with those who maybe we don't care for nearly as much.

As a critical care physician, I work in a professionally competitive world in which there is little time for facades and where emotions run high. I hope the professional and personal insights I have gained and the things I have learned the hard way, will help you cope with the more difficult moments of life and avoid some of the pitfalls I have experienced.

Finally, I really hope these verses will help you feel free to celebrate who you are, build your understanding of your own strengths, the dimensions in which you are not so strong and that it will help you cope with both.

Write What You Know

Everyone says, "Write what you know."
I know what it's like to see in people their good,
I know what it's like to be misunderstood.

I know what it's like, in people to believe,
I know what it's like to be deceived.

I know what it's like, with dogs to play.
I know what it's like to hear what they say.

I know what it's like to have intuition,
I know what it's like to have inhibitions.

I know what it's like to create.
I know what it's like to live with heartbreak.

I know what it's like to live for love's sake,
I know what it's like to love until my heart breaks.

I know what it's like to give all I can.
I know what it's like to live, without a set-in stone plan.

I know what it's like to play a role.
I know what it's like to do as I am told.

And though I will never quite tell,
I know what it's like to rebel.

Know Who You Are

So many people will happily tell you who you are,
Even if they have only seen you from afar.
Afraid to compare;
To really see you, they do not dare.

They cast you in whatever light
Gives them delight.
Their mission is to denigrate,
Until you disintegrate.

A need to gossip
'Til you feel sick.
A need to paint
In any way that taints.
And while you were never a saint,
You don't need to be reformed,
But now, you hear your life transformed;
And it cuts you to the quick.

A made-up life.
The removal of all accomplishments,
Must be your punishment.
A life full of strife.
The restoration of your reputation,
Must be your solitary preoccupation.

Let them say what they may.
Don't let them bring you to tears,

With their smears and their jeers.
Understand your fears.
Don't let them make you regret
Stuff you didn't do,
Things you didn't get.
Do not stray
And become who they say.

Live your life, knowing you are unique.
Live your life, knowing what you seek.
Understand what makes your mind sing;
Forget the sting
Of people who only bring misery and pain,
As their constant refrain.

Do not get cast into their mold.
Let your real self unfold.
Do not let them demean,
For you are *far* more than ever you seem.

Remember your potential is beyond belief.
Ignore such people, it will be such a relief.
Live your life in self-discovery,
Not in self-recovery.

The Perfect Reply

Where do you see yourself in five years?
In Ten?
Part of me wishes I could actually answer them.
Tell me about yourself in a five minute elevator ride.
God! I find that question so very snide.

If you are asking who I am
And for what I stand,
Then let's sit for a while
And I will tell you what makes me smile.
And for what I will walk a thousand miles.

What do I see when I look in the mirror?
Well… it's the messy parts of life,
That make **me** so much clearer.

From the mess,
From the way I handle stress.
When things are not as planned;
When I must take a stand.

Through strengths and weaknesses I define;
My sense of self is constantly refined.
On this journey of self-discovery
And constant recovery,
From the times when I was not so strong,
From the moments when I was wrong.

So, please do not frown
At my request to sit down.
Your questions need to stop,
For life should not be so cropped.
For, do you *not* see?
It should not be planned from A to Z.

It is in the unexpected parts
That my life truly starts.
It is in the unpredicted spaces
Where magic and grace is.

To your questions and any similar query,
I do have a set and tightly worded reply.
Yet… I just get so weary
And my disinterest in you I cannot hide,
If you now persist in questions so snide.

For in the end,
I am more interesting than
What can be told,
What can be sold
In your five minute elevator ride.

So Smart

What is it like to be so smart?
You may as well ask
And begin the task,
Of tearing me apart.

Instead of seeing me,
You dissect my mind.
And all that really makes me, me
Is conveniently left behind.

What is it like to be so smart?
What information do you want me to impart?
Please tell me what you mean;
I am exactly what I seem.

Yes, I am often lost in thought
And I speak, when maybe I should not.
But I am still often fraught
With emotions, like any other,
For which there is no cover.
And I too, struggle to make sense
Of my life's more challenging events.

What is it like to be so smart?
Well… here is the wisdom I will share,
Because I will take life's dare.
Being smart is being kind.
Being smart is realising a rare find.
Being smart is taking an interest in all things
In the tremendous beauty to be found,
In life all around.

Overlooked

Smart people are often overlooked.
People often prefer the cover of a book
And complicated content,
Doesn't make them content.

'You can't judge a book by its cover'
Is a saying of yore.
That doesn't seem to hold true anymore.
Contextualisation
Demands too much visualisation.

Smart people are forced to dissemble,
To others resemble.
Forced to please
By being less than they seem.
Trying to fit in,
Their minds to trim.

Yet why play this part?
If you are meant to stand apart,
Why follow the herd?
If you are meant to be heard,
Why try to blend in?
When that would be a sin.

What do you gain?
Except so much pain.
Why live like this?
Just to exist.

Be yourself instead.
Let go of your dread
And celebrate what's in your head.
There is nothing wrong with being smart
And, in this way, standing apart.

Worst Enemy

Don't be your own worst enemy;
You have plenty of frenemies for that.
They will be more than happy
To give you tit for tat;
It's not at all hard to see that.

Instead, see your faults.
As your personal default settings,
The inputs you'll be getting,
Will be the seeds you sow;
To help you grow.

Don't be your own worst enemy.
From others you are no different,
Though they would have you believe they are magnificent.
Do not be scared of being weak,
Though it is strength you always seek.

Do not run away, stay.
Why do you not believe the words I say?
Brimming with wealth,
You will find yourself
When you see,
Exactly who you can be.

Social Media

Unsure how to feel,
Unsure how to deal
With a complicated world.
Your mind in a whirl.

To social media you turn.
So many people of all ages
Telling the ins and outs of their every moment, on its pages.

Total strangers tell you how to feel.
Total strangers tell you how to deal.
Emotions amplified, swirl,
"This one will make you positively sob."
Of any thoughts of your own, robbed.
Anger burns,
Your mind churns.

Why is it the thoughts and emotions of others you possess?
Why is it so important to be liked online?
How is this a productive use of your time?
Why don't you look up from your screen
And assess
The world as it is?
Not as they would have you believe.

People who know Everything

They brazenly state their claim
To every domain.
Their game is clear;
To demean all, far and near.

Their misperceived superiority rankles all around.
What pleasure do they get from running others down?
And when they are proven wrong,
Grin! They just argue all the more strong!

They think they are demonstrating their skill,
With their voices so shrill.
Yet their need to display their superiority
Countermands their authority.

Instead of thinking they know so much
A truly superior intellect will pause to reflect,
Learn from those who know more,
Understand there is no need to keep score.

For it is people who are as such
Who really do know
much.

Those who display honour and grace.
Those who do not see a race.
Those who accept when they do not know.
Those who have no need to put on a show.
They are the smartest ones of all;
The ones who see shame
In such a game.

Who You Know

All you can talk about is who you know.
Isn't it exhausting to put on such a show?

The implication is that you get favours
That will help you live a life you savour,
From people well placed
And it will win you the race.

Why do you name drop so much?
Do you believe their names bring you luck?

Flip the coin around and reveal
Why should they care about you
And how you feel?
Do they know you use their names like this?
Do they really know you exist?

Do you really think
Such people will save you from the brink?
They are much more apt to let you sink.

Seriously, what is the big deal?
This is how I feel.

Two Faces

You are so two-faced,
How can anyone keep pace?
Speaking from both sides of your mouth.
Don't you know sooner or later it will all go south?

You flatter,
As though time doesn't matter.
The next moment you foment
And your words torment
The very ones you flattered.
What, in God's name, with you is the matter?

Are you looking for secondary gain,
When you cause so much pain?
Do you live off people's remains,
As you watch them live in chains?
Seriously, just *what* do you gain?

Work

Some people are defined by the work they do.
Tell me, is that you?

Some people are only interested in the money they earn.
Tell me, do you have enough money to burn?
Will you be taking it with you in your urn?

Some people brag they haven't taken time to read a book in years.
Such statements, made with pride, nearly reduce me to tears.

In a world so vast,
When life is over so fast,
How can your interest not be found in everything surround?

When you retire, will you have nothing to do?
Will you know you?
Who will you find?
Will you be of sound mind?

Disguise

Some have a public face
For public spaces.
So many disguise
All their lies.
The look in their eyes,
Always polite
To everyone in sight.

For some, a public face is unknown,
Emotions free to roam,
For all to see
Instantly.

Outer voices
That make no choices.
Why does it seem
That so many people, don't say what they mean?

And when you speak true,
You are told it's your inner voice poking through.
The message to quell
Any truths you try to tell.
How long has it been,
Since someone can't say what they mean?

Honesty is a sin.
Lies make so much din.
Where are we all going
When no truth is showing?

Perfectionist

You are a perfectionist.
There is no detail too small for you to miss.
You drive everyone crazy,
For you do not tolerate the slightest detail being hazy.
Your appearance even says it all.
Mirror, mirror on the wall,
You are the most perfect of them all.

There is nothing wrong
With attention to detail holding strong.
At this, you are the best
And, in the dust, leave all the rest.

But your drive to succeed
Brings everyone to their knees.
But in your drive to achieve,
Your standards aren't always necessary to succeed.

Being a perfectionist is not a crime.
You aren't even doing it by design.
But know your desire to achieve heights,
Does cause others to take flight.

Ask yourself what details can you let go?
Which do you have to maintain
For it not to show?
For it not to drive you insane?

Sometimes just a bit of letting go is okay.
Trust that it won't destroy your day.
Sometimes just a bit of letting go,
Will let your life and that of those around you slow
And everyone's creativity will grow.

Don't drive everyone to exhaustion;
Use caution.
Be more sensitive to the standards you set.
You may be happily surprised by the results you get.

Fake People

Fake people, with their personal fake news abound.
It's so hard to find authenticity in this town.
Fake people with fake expressions of caring.
How can they be so daring?

So many people worm their way in,
Under your skin,
Into your life,
Only to use you
And abuse you.
And it's just not right.

Self-glorification in full stride;
Is something broken inside?
What is it about yourself you can't abide?
What is this need to be so dramatic?
To live so fantastic?

A beam of light;
The sun doesn't even burn as bright.
Drop the acts.
Live within real facts.
If you don't care move on;
Stop stringing people along.

Where has your reality been?
When was your truth last seen?
It's time to try authenticity.

Drop your complicity —
Your life will be smaller
But you will stand taller.
And just maybe then, a grin
Will begin
And you will truly smile,
For a very long while.

I am SOOO Busy

"I am sooo busy," is your constant refrain;
The mirage you feel you must sustain
As you socialise
And weave sooo many lies.

For you would rather go for a drink,
Than think
And then work yourself to the brink.
Sooo many lies.
All these efforts to hypnotise.

You hardly have time to sleep
And others, for you, just weep.
No life of your own
Sigh! You are simply just never at home!

Imagine so many people's surprise,
If they could see through your disguise.
Imagine your surprise
If, instead of speaking in tongues,
You actually got things done!
If instead of empty words,
You took action.
Why, just imagine your own satisfaction!

Words without Actions

Many say words are cheap,
That it's actions you must seek.
But are they themselves just sheep?

Words reveal truths to be told.
Actions are how you are seen to be bold.

Flowery words and promises are all amiss.
Words and actions must align.
If not, it's a sign
That should not be maligned,
By anyone in their right mind.

Words without action
Bring no satisfaction.
They are just lies
That beget many sighs.
Life is over too fast
For your words alone to last.

Fill the Air

Words fill your air.
So many words, I am scared.
Words everywhere
Yet meaning not there.

You don't pause to breathe
And my mind just seethes,
As your words from one subject to another fly.
Incoherent,
Inconsistent;
Their emptiness steals my sky.

Are you nervous?
Or simply impervious?
Do you realise?
Should I sympathise?

Why do you continue to speak?
Is it for the thrill?
You are not demonstrating any skill
And, somewhere deep inside, it makes me want to kill.

Silence is not overrated
Though your words continue, unabated.

A Book

How has it become a creed?
Pride, in a land where no one reads.
What pride should ever be took,
That no one has ever cracked a book?

People don't read anymore.
Lost in superficiality,
Even out of touch with reality.
A depth of thought lost,
A terrible cost.
Such a horror
We have all become poorer.

Concepts not mentioned,
Lead to misapprehension
And create tension.

The whole story never told.
A bill of goods sold.
Concepts simplified
To keep the story alive.
On the internet, such stories you will find.
It's enough to blow your mind.

In contrast, in books lost in nooks and crooks;
Vast explorations of meanings,
Expansionistic leanings.
More complexity of thought
Then could ever be sought.
Plenty of adventures to find
To develop and feed your mind.

Whether reason or rhyme,
A book will take you across borders and through time.
So, tell me now what pride should ever be took
That until now, you have never cracked a book?

Words that Matter

Words that matter
Don't necessarily flatter.
They cut to the bone
To overcome thoughts that roam.
They seek to speak truths,
Without any ruse.

They ask you to see the world's true light,
Away from those who can't bear to see you burn bright.
Away from those who don't want you to find
The answers in your own mind.

They seek instead, to explore what races through your head,
When you lie in bed.
They seek to help you cope
At times when it's only human to lose hope.
They ask you to question who you are.
They ask you what and where is your North Star.
They tell you, you are not alone.
They tell you, you are home.

Words in Text/Email

Beyond the pale
Is your email.
Destruction in its path,
The only aftermath.

Abrupt is not concise
And to be concise,
Does not politeness slice.

Words paint pictures.
Words convey meaning.
Words either prevent or promote conjectures.
Words either prevent or promote dreaming.

Careless texts deployed
Are relationships destroyed.
Typed words in emails and texts
Are never devoid of context
And it's ridiculous, to think in these formats alone.
Typed words are devoid of tone.

Emails and texts are not an excuse
To be rude and play obtuse.
Emails and texts do have tone;
Be very careful of your own.

On the spectrum of welcome and rejection,
Where are you forming your connection?
Say what you mean
And make sure it's exactly what it seems.

Bullies

Bullies like to keep everyone under their thumb.
Bullies think everyone else is dumb.
The reign of misery,
Positively gives them glee.

It's easy for them to succeed.
They propagate like weeds.
They thrive on maleficent power
Like some munificent flower.

They seek to destroy
All there is to enjoy,
Yet as they instigate
Their hate.
What do they ever create?

There is no way to deal with them, that is tried and true.
But I will say this to you:
Their power is much reduced,
When you share.
Their power is much reduced,
If others say, "N*ow stop right there!*"
Their power is much reduced,
When you don't care.

Leaders

Leaders are often anointed
When they should be appointed.
Leaders are too often chosen, among people who could,
Through their connections,
And not among those who should.
For this would defy current conventions.

The results I have found
Is they live to tear others down.
Instead of building others up,
They tell them to just shut up.

Those who lead, ought to know
That for their skills to show,
Leaders have to have vision
And quell division.

A leader real and true
Will appreciate you,
Mentor and help you achieve.
Revel in the accolades you receive
Without jealousy or reservation.
They will celebrate your creations.
For this is how leaders build their own small nations.

So, tell me what kind of leader are you?
Even if anointed,
In the end you have a choice,
As to how you use your voice.

Truth To Power

Isolated in their tower:
Power.
Surrounded by people who say, "Yes."
Why? It's not hard to guess.

Seen as a test
That no one contests.
Seen as a pest
If someone should protest.
With compliments and gifts showered:
Power.

When they talk
Far too many cower:
Power.

Echoes off stones.
Effectively all alone,
Cut off from the ground.
Only flattered by all around:
Power.

Yet one person alone can only have so much vision,
Without a need for some derision.
Not every idea is good.
Be the little engine that could,
Don't be a wallflower.
Speak truth to power.

Silenced

It is your area of expertise,
Yet they do not ask you to speak.
You are not even asked to chair a session
On the topic that is your obsession.

It is normal to feel betrayed
And ask, is there a reason they are trying to make you pay?
Are they jealous?
Or is it just your discomfort they relish?
Especially when their chosen get it wrong
And you feel like it's the same old song.
Especially when you are asked, *"Why aren't you speaking?*
Is the event too small for the fame you are seeking?"

An expert comes to build collaboration with a visit.
Since the expert is a friend, your happiness is exquisite.
But you are not invited to the dinner, though I suppose it's no surprise.
Why are you anathematised?
If a bored colleague hadn't eventually stepped aside,
You wouldn't even have caught a moment by his side.
But you are apparently expected to take this all in stride.

Having lived far too many of these moments,
Of these torments,
There are decisions to make.
Two choices at stake:
Live with people such as this, ruling your fate,

Learn to hate
Or, when it begins,
Though it's hard, learn to not let them win.
Live with people for whose opinion you care.
Learn to ignore petty snares.
Live with people whose knowledge you share.

Blocked

What do you do when you have writer's block?
What do you do when you don't have a thought?
Or when they all swirl around
Never to come aground?

Well... I cast around.
Are there topics to define?
Concepts to refine?
Do I have anything to contribute?
Are there concepts I need to refute?
Is there meaning to glean
From things I have seen?

Then, I devise a plan to struggle
To make sense of all this muddle
And really... for something to say.
I just think about my day.
What did I learn?
What made my mind burn?

Silver Linings

Why are you whining?
Just look for the silver lining
In all life's events, big and small.
Don't you know, there is one in them all?

I don't believe this is actually true.
Tell me — honestly now, do you?
Sometimes, life's events are just not good and even downright sad,
Sometimes, some days are just clearly bad.

Stop your pining.
Look for the silver lining.
Might be words meant to bolster
On life's rollercoaster
But silver linings don't always exist
And it doesn't help anyone's coping, to persist
For a failure to find.
Ends just being another failure in your mind.

Sometimes, life is only full of thorns
On which we all get torn,
Is truth unadorned.
There may be no silver lining
But nor is a warrant of despair,
What you need to be sighting.

Terrible, awful and sad days, we all have them.
Try not to feel completely downtrodden
And, by a happier world, forgotten.

Sometimes the only thing such moments do teach,
Is some resilience to prepare for the next breach,
Their details still searing.
Try to close your eyes without them alone, being all you are seeing.
Or at least figure out how you can cope
And how not to lose hope.

No one can promise better days around the bend.
But know, most of the time, such moments do end.

Because it's 20_ _

The Old Boys' club is alive and just swell.
Rumours to the contrary, let me quickly dispel.
Because it's 20 _ _ is said loud and clear
But do you see any real differences, my dear?

The Old Boys' Club is alive and swell.
Don't be cast under publicity's spell.
No matter how they sin,
They almost always win.
Gender
Remains one of the world's tenders.

Backroom meetings, private greetings.
Differences in status now covert.
All still designed to effectively subvert,
Like phoenixes rising.
Frankly, it actually is quite surprising.

Any leadership positions assigned,
Are positions less valued
And consume more time.
Positions of low worth
Given, by others, a very wide berth.
But you are expected
To be honoured, excited, connected, respected

Because it's 20 _ _ is said loud and shrill.
But my dear, do you not feel the chill?

Positions less visible,
Authority in decision-making less accessible.
At the end of the day,
Who do you sway?
No real seat at the table.
Yet often, much more able.

Token positions without a real voice,
Should never be an acceptable choice.
What does gender have to do with knowledge, skill or ability?
Why do gender-based perceptions provoke any ego fragility?
Why does gender-based arrogance exist?
How is society just when, with such force, change it resists?

When does inequality end?
Why is it so hard to comprehend?
Isn't it time for us all to grow up and real partnerships form?
Because it's 20 _ _, why isn't this the norm?

Glass Ceiling

The competition is fierce
For the top tier to pierce.
Many will so repeatedly say
To keep your ambition at bay.

The competition is fierce
For the top tier to pierce.
Many will want to make you believe
That *this* success, you can't achieve.

Don't let their negativity
Crush your creativity.
Do not be overwhelmed.
Be the captain at your own helm:
Raise your mast,
Sail on past.

Write with Rage

Write with RAGE
Pouring onto every page.
When something isn't right,
Don't let the issues scatter.
Injustice always matters.

Write with RAGE
Pouring onto every page.
Injustices always start small,
Then you find your back against the wall.
Pick up your pen and write.
Harness your rage and fight.

Write with RAGE
Pouring onto every page.
For change then, WRITE,
Don't settle, don't be trite,
Become a LIGHT.

Humanitarian Work

Why do you do humanitarian work?
Do you not have enough,
With all your other stuff?

Don't you see?
It's important to me
To right the wrongs I can,
To even take a stand.

Too much injustice to be found.
Lost in the world where too often, it makes no sound.
Someone has to try to level the ground.

Imagine what the world *could* be.
Don't you *see?*
Why not me?!

Last Words of Your Life

Don't you find it concerning?
Even disturbing:
The magnification of being great,
The CV to constantly update,
The deletion of the slightest mistake,
As though their life is at stake.

In verity,
Why do they care so much for their own posterity?
Banting and Best
Invented insulin, no less.
Yet now, it's anyone's guess.
And it's such a shame,
That no one can remember their names.

Leaving the world better than you found it,
That should be what keeps you grounded.
The last words of your life
Should not be, "I published in the __ __ __ thrice."

Don't you see?
I really don't know about you,
But I would rather my last words to be
I love you
And thank you for loving me.
Then bring my ashes to the river.
Gently let me go
Into its current's soft flow.

Part of water's sparkling glow
Part of the lives of others
As they walk its shores.
Part of the lives of lovers
Forevermore.

Nerves of Steel

Dealing with so many moments of torment,
You have become as tough as nails,
Just to not go off the rails.

Nerves of steel,
You reveal.
Tell me, are you ever allowed to feel?

A tough outer shell,
So no one can tell.
You have been so torn apart
That you have even lost heart.

Nerves of steel,
You reveal.
Tell me, what would happen if you began to feel?

Years of service, years of forgiving.
Crossing a bridge too far, now beginning.
Tell me what is inside.
Tell me, what do you hide?

Nerves of steel,
You reveal.
Now tell me, what is happening as you begin to feel?

Our History

Rewriting our history,
Revising what you believed.
Telling you it's all lies
And not to believe your own eyes.

Things need to stay where they were.
Facts need to concur
Otherwise life becomes a fairy-tale
And these don't all end well.

Even if our history is rife
With facts not so nice,
Life should remain non-fiction
And reality, society's addiction.

With us, our history we carry.
We need to learn, not bury.
Don't put our history away on a shelf,
Instead let's look at it squarely
And see how and where people were treated unfairly,
When it wasn't nice,
When it was full of vice.
See it as a call
For us to avoid our next fall.

Courage

What would it take
To be the first bird to sing,
When there is yet, no certainty of spring?

What would it take
To be the one leaf, that refuses to change colour
When the fading light of autumn, changes all others?

What would it take
To be the one flower that blooms,
When winter's harsh cold looms?

What would it take
To be the one, whose voice rings out loud
When all others follow the crowd?

What would it take
To be the one, who stands braver
When all others waiver?

Shhhh!

Let your guard down.
There is no one else around.
Trust in what you see;
Trust in me.

For the secrets you conceal,
I will never reveal.
In love, all is fair
And our love is without compare.

Trust in what you feel.
Know my love is real
And that I will never reveal,
The secrets you conceal.

Smile

With a broad smile,
People you beguile.

With such a simple switch,
People are bewitched.

A way through any storm.
A day transformed.
A joy for everyone:
The rising of the sun.

For nothing can replace
A smile on your face.

Stare at the Sky

Go stand outside and stare at the sky.
Go stand outside and wonder, why?

Vast and calm,
It is held in your palm.

Vast and dramatic,
It is simply fantastic.

Vast and solemn,
It is its own poem.

Vast and sweeping,
It is mysteries keeping.

Go stand outside and stare at the sky.
Harness the child inside.
Open your eyes wide.
Go stand outside and wonder, why?

Why is your heart aglow?
What do you need to grow?

In the melody of your mind,
What will you find?

Waiting for a Prince

Why do you wait for a Prince?
Why do you need to be told
That you have a heart of gold?

Why do you wait for a Prince?
Is it *so* important to have and to hold?
Life is not a fairy tale to be told.

Is it true love you are seeking?
Beware of the words you are speaking.
If it is true love you are seeking,
Beware of the company you are keeping.

Who you know and what you have
Are foundations, crumbling.
Who you are is thunder rumbling.

Be bold.
Your future should not be sold.
Why do you wait for a Prince?

A Bad Relationship

What the F----?
When will you stop passing the buck?
When will you take responsibility?
When will I get to live, without hostility?

I am not a doll you take off the shelf.
You only think of yourself.
Don't be such a narcissist;
I am worth much more than this.

If you truly value me,
Then why don't you try to see
What it's like, to really be me?

Why don't you try to actually care?
Will you take my dare?

Time to Leave

I sit and write in the mountain air.
I sit and write without a care.
I sit and write though my fingers freeze.
God, there is such a wintry breeze!

But I must write this down,
For new wisdom I have found.

The stories you tell
Cast quite a spell.
My emotions I must quell,
So I don't go through hell.

I know people will talk.
But it's time for me to walk.
I may have been wrong,
But now, NOW I am strong!

Single

You are pretty fun and smart.
Why hasn't a man snatched you up?
C'mon, tell me what's up.
Wouldn't it be sweet?
Wouldn't you feel more complete?

Well… for a start.
I am smart.
For better or worse is often a curse.
To have and to hold is often being told.
What does pretty and fun
Have to do with needing someone?

How do you bear to own your own home?
Doesn't it feel empty and alone?
What happens if something breaks down?
Wouldn't it be easier to have a man around?

Well… if something needs to be fixed,
I can figure it out pretty quick.
I am practical
And rational
And if I can't fix it alone,
I can figure out who to phone.

But you love to travel and it isn't safe for a woman to traipse
All over the place.
Wouldn't you feel less alone, if you had someone to share

Your every care?

Well… great friends are a wealth
Who also care, in sickness and health.
Being alone in different places,
Doesn't mean I don't know what safe is.

With books to read and those to write.
Things to learn; for nothing is black and white.
My violin to play and it has plenty to say.
Dogs to walk and they love to talk.
I could go on and on
But time is running long.
I always find so much to do,
Why can't you?

If a man fits into all this,
I agree it could be bliss.
But pardon my reservations
On this topic of our conversation.
Frankly, there is no need for a man
For me, to know who I am.

Roots tangled around stone.
The tree that so grows is still at home.
In its wilder mind and untamed beauty,
Resilience is both its story and its glory.
A sentinel growing atop its rock
Defies convention, without stop.
Though it may, at times, be lonely,
Not told it couldn't, in this way, live,

Losing its independence would be quite a price to give.

Roots tightly tangled around stone,
Do not a make a beggar on a throne.
Though there is a certain ferocity
In its life's luminosity,
Being on your own
Doesn't mean being alone.

Holding On

Do not hold on too tightly.
You will not like the vibrations,
The screams of the spirit nations
And you will lose connection
With creation.

Do not hold on too slightly.
Your thoughts will not burn brightly
And the damage will be unsightly.

Hold on gently.
Listen and learn what it takes to grow
And not to fear moonlight's glow.

A Break

In the world today,
Voices never cease
And leave your brow permanently creased.
Every which way, tossed by the wind,
Peace you rescind.

Rushing around,
Your life upside down.
Against the current rowing,
Even more stress is showing.

Rest for a moment.
Release your mind from all its torment.
Lay down your oars.
Listen as the violin soars.

The Country

You get claustrophobic in the city.
Ivory towers
Without bowers,
People all around,
No peace to be found.

Born in the woods,
You moved away when you should.
Moved from sunshine, dappling trees and ferns,
Thinking it was just a natural life turn.

Life changes
And re-arranges.
You feel your city time is done,
Though there have been times of fun.
You are starting to crack.
Leave, don't look back.

A return to the country.
Asked by all and sundry,
How people can live?
What do the woods have to give?

Doesn't boredom set in
And get under your skin?
How do you live here
When nothing is near?

How do you make this your home?
How do you not feel so alone?
How do you resist the will to roam,
When the woods, you call home?

It is not that hard to comprehend,
When the woods and all within are your friends.
The light-hearted ferns, waving in the breeze,
The depths of forest greens and tangled roots,
The softness underfoot
Ever changing,
Yet unwavering.

Adventures without need to embellish.
Laughter and caring without contrivance flourish.
Resilient and resolute,
Impossible now for this to refute.
I will not stand down.
It's in the woods I am found.

Liberation

Last night, I wrote by candlelight
With a fountain pen.
There is nothing like a failure of electricity,
A return to simplicity;
Life is calmer, then.

Lost in time.
Lost in rhyme.
Is that a crime?

Away from distraction
Is not a subtraction.
Lost in deliberation
Is a salvation.

Tomorrow

Not today, but tomorrow.
Life is full of too much sorrow.
When what should be said today,
Is left for another day,
As though there is nothing left to say.

I never told you
Just how much you mean to me.
I never trusted you.
I never let you see,

Who I am
Without disguise.
For fear
You wouldn't recognise,
The one you keep so near,
The one you hold so dear.

Not today, but tomorrow.
Life is full of too much sorrow.
If only I had let you see what's in my heart.
Would I now be so torn apart?

What do I Miss?

What is it about you I miss?
The way your smile
Burned through the gloom
And lit up the room.

The way your delight
In all things, even slight,
Burned so bright
It often kept you awake all night.

The way you could make me laugh
At the silliest of things.
The way you could remove all the world's stings.

The way we would talk
When we went on those walks.
When everything made sense,
Though the world was no different.

Nature

The blaze of glory's light.
Why for you, does it not still burn bright?

How can you not stop
And look at beauty surround?
In the forests it abounds.
How can you not see
The simple reality of its complexity?

I sit in the forest and listen to its beat.
Do you not feel the warmth of its cedar's heat?
Do you not hear its voice?
Or is it simply a matter of choice?

A Simple Spring

Bare branches like lace intertwined,
Memories of passing time.

Teasing sultry scents breezes bring.
In sunshine, hearts sing.

Speckled snow clings to grass,
Too tired and old to last.

Walking on diamond mines.
Salt on pavement still shines.

Chapters close.
It's time for a new, blood-red rose.

The Loon cries Low

When the loon cries low
In the afternoon glow.

When life is no longer a stage
And the sunset's gaze
Sets the waves ablaze.

Put your phone down,
Lie on the warm ground,
Listen to other sounds;
Peace has been found.

Breathe in deep.
Feel your heart begin to weep.
Feel your memories sweep away;
Live for today.
Feel your mind begin to unwind;
Isn't it about time?

When time loses meaning…
And you can hear your heart beating.
Just remember to think slow,
When the loon cries low.

November Rain

How can you ever be the same,
After walking in the November rain?

Trees stripped of their fiery glories,
Dripping with water crystals, telling different stories.

Listen to the soft quiet of the trees.
The person who listens, really sees.

Don't worry about the next rhyme.
Don't look for any sign.
Feel like you are walking back through time.

The Child Inside

Where does the child go,
When you begin to grow?
The cult of being adult,
Buries the child within
Under layers far from thin.

The awe of possibility,
To see beyond reality.
The joy to venture,
To see beyond conjecture.
The insights beyond perception,
To see beyond question.
The sense of mystery,
To see beyond history.
The insatiable quest for why.
To see way, way, up into the sky.
Can you still find the child's wide-eye wonder,
Peeking out from under?

Glimpses of the child can surely still be seen:
Eyes sparkling, gleam,
Standing off in the waiting wings,
Caught in the shadows, waiting for a new spring,
Draped in a blanket, toes poking through,
Sucking on a thumb,
Staring, in wonder, at what it has become.

Sanctuary

A sanctuary is shared
When love is laid bare.

Against all the world's assaults
And despite my many faults,
When I need to vent,
When I need to repent,
When I suspect
That I am far from perfect.
You let me be me,
You make me feel free;
Sanctuary.

Throughout all life's troubles,
Even when I feel reduced to rubble.
Somehow you are always there,
Somehow you still care
At the end of every day.
The look I always want to see
Is the one you reserve just for me;
Sanctuary.

You tell me on inspection,
I will not find perfection.
Sometimes you defy convention,
Other times you will need redemption.
You are simply you:
Someone decent and true.

Sanctuary.

You can tell me everything, you say.
I am that person for you
And you are that person for me.
Do you not see?
Open your mind to me
And I will share mine completely.
Sanctuary.

Do you know how much that means at the end of the day?
Well, it means far more than I can ever say.
Having *that* person to trust implicitly
Is simplicity
Unbound
And rarely found.

A marriage of hearts
Is not what sets us apart.
A marriage of minds
Is the most essential sign
Of a love of the deepest kind.

No matter where life leads.
No matter how our hearts bleed.
Love is love when it sees clearly
And I love you, so incredibly dearly.
A sanctuary is shared
When love is laid bare.

What Matters in the End

What matters in the end,
Is who you choose as a friend.
If friends are the family you choose
There is so much more to lose.
With no binding ties,
No need to believe any of your lies,
Bonds can be torn
Before each and every morn.

Popularity is often the trend,
When people seek friends.
Yet a real friend doesn't like you for name dropping sake.
Quite the reverse, otherwise they're fake.

For others, friendship is a flower,
They gloat at over every hour.
As they flit from one to another,
Who will they discover?
What will they uncover?
For sampling every flower
For them is power.

Real friends understand your dread,
The childhood monsters that still haunt your head.
In misery, they commiserate
And reassure you, it's not fate.
They will get you through each and every December.
They will help you remember.

When you are troubled,
When you are in a muddle,
They hold on tight.
They get you through the night.
They remain steadfast,
For that is how friendships last.

Real friends share your delight.
They bring both sight and light.
For what matters in the end
Is who you call friend.

Thank You for What You Do

Thank you for what you do,
Are words heard by so very few.
These are words we should all hear more,
Instead of the closing of the door.

Gracious thanks for your outstanding contributions:
When configured in your daily resolutions
Are words meaningful,
Thoughtful,
People illuminating
And even exhilarating.

The people I admire most
Do not hesitate to sincerely say
Such words every day.
Each day rendered:
Sparkling, special and splendid.
An abundance of joy, peace and contentment created.
Really, the effect of saying, "Thanks," can't be overstated.

The people I admire most,
Understand the most fundamental of truths.
A few kind words can turn a life around.
A few kind words in beauty surround.

Thanks for all you so fabulously do.
Let these words be heard by so many more, than just a few.
Take time to show you have class.
Live every day as though it's your last

Find Yourself

Find yourself on these pages.
Find yourself through the ages.
Do you see yourself clear?
Do you see the ones you hold dear?

Find yourself in these stories.
See your present and former glories.
Find your faults and worst traits.
Distance will help you see straight.

Leave behind
All the parts you would rather not find.
Grow and be kind,
For you are here in every line.
Do you not see the signs?

Fall Where They May

Too many people let words fall where they may,
Unconcerned about their meaning
Even if they are demeaning.

Pay more attention.
Clearly state your intentions.
Words carelessly thrown
When facts are unknown,
Lead to too much hurt
Even if it's covert.

So heed
What you say.
Hold your words at bay.
Realise your comments
Affect others' moments.
So, do not let them fall where they may.
For how can you not know,
You reap what you sow?

The Power of Verse

It's easier to remember a verse
Than a curse.

I hope these will make you smile
For a long while.

I hope these will make you reflect,
On what you want to protect.

I hope these will bring you light
And even some delight.

I hope these words help you cope,
When you lose hope.

I hope these words matter

And do remember this:
A curse can often make things so much worse
Than a verse.

www.ingramcontent.com/pod-product-compliance
Lightning Source LLC
LaVergne TN
LVHW041538060526
838200LV00037B/1042